MW01026125

A Guide To European Christmas Markets

Christmas Markets In Europe, Where To Go, What To See & Markets Schedule 2022-2023

Carol Bell

CONTENTS

INTRODUCTION

Celebrating Advent and the Christmas season is one of Europe's longest traditions. But these days it's more than just a tradition. Christmas is a social event for friends and family to get together after work or on the weekends leading up to Christmas Day and often includes time spent at the local Christmas market.

With the aroma of hot spiced wine, roasted sausages, and nuts filling the air, there's no better way to get into the holiday spirit than by visiting a Christmas market. Nestled in city squares across Germany, Austria, Switzerland, France, and beyond, these markets are filled with ornately decorated stalls selling hand-painted glass ornaments, delicious seasonal food, and all-around yuletide cheer.

I've been fortunate to spend time in Europe, where visiting the Christmas markets is a winter highlight. In this guide, I share my views on the best Christmas markets in Europe for 2022. But before that, let's take a very short history lesson.

Short history

Europe's Christmas markets are steeped in history. The first market was said to be held in Vienna, Austria dating back to 1296, but the first "winter market" was in Munich, Germany in 1310. The first "official" market was Dresden's Strietzelmarkt in 1434.

Christmas markets are also known as Christkindlmarkt, Christkindlesmarkt, Christkindlmarket, Christkindlimarkt, and Weihnachtsmarkt and take place during the start of Advent.

Each market has it's own traditions, decorations, and food. Germany's markets tend to be more traditional while Austria's tend to be a bit more elaborate.

Most markets end just before Christmas, but in towns such as Speyer, Germany they prolong the celebration. You'll see lovely stalls (or chalets) selling handcrafted ornaments and crafts, local food, and hot, mulled wine called glühwein.

First things first...

Avoid the crowds: Europeans take Christmas markets very seriously. Avoid crowds and lines by going during the day, or opt for going during the week, Mondays or Tuesdays are best.

Good To Know

Many of the stalls selling glühwein (and some food) will have something called a "pfand" this is extra money that you'll pay for the cup, usually a few euros. Once done with your drink you can keep the cup (usually they are a great souvenir as they say the location and date) or return it to get your money back.

Bring cash, most sellers will only take cash at a Christmas market. The winter markets can be cold, so make sure to bring something warm and comfortable shoes. You'll most likely be on your feet to peruse the stalls.

Most major European cities have Christmas markets, and they are all lovely. But, I have been to dozens so I'm pulling out the best Christmas markets to get the "real" experience along with an itinerary to help you on your way.

Your European Christmas Market Route

Fly into Germany – I suggest Frankfurt. This is a major airport hub and makes it easy to go to your next destination. From here, you can take a train or a car (I find cars are easiest and make it so you can stop off at any time). From here, take a train or car to Heidelberg, Germany.

This is a typical Christmas market and will put you right in the spirit. Next, we're heading to France! Strasbourg is only about an hour and a half away from Heidelberg.

After you get your fill of Glühwein our next stop is still in Alsace: Colmar, France. An actual gingerbread town, it's one of the cutest places I've ever stepped foot in!

After France we'll cross another border and head into Switzerland. Here we'll go to Basel then Bern and if time permits we'll go to Lucerne and back north to Zurich. This itinerary is perfect if you have 5-7 days.

Have more time, or just want to see more? Keep on going! From here you can go back into Germany for Munich's markets or go straight over to Austria. If you're driving, stop off in Salzburg. But since this is a long journey, I suggest flying to Vienna. Next you can either head to Prague (my personal favorite) or east to Budapest.

CHAPTER ONE

Dresden Christmas Market 2022 – Dates: 23 Nov To 24 Dec

Germany has so many wonderful Christmas markets but if I had to choose the very best, it would be Dresden Christmas Market. You can't beat the incredible beauty of Dresden's baroque Old Town (Altstadt) with the rebuilt Frauenkirche, Brühl's Terraces, the Opera and the incredible Zwinger.

The Christmas markets in Dresden are the oldest in Europe and probably the biggest in

Germany. Let's get to look at some of them.

Dresden Christmas Market 2022

The long history of the Striezelmarkt is unmatched and today you have a huge variety of Christmas markets from the traditional Frauenkirche Christmas market to the quieter Romantic Christmas Market.

Location: Striezelmarkt is located at Altmarkt but there are several other Advent markets in Dresden.

Reason to visit: The Striezelmarkt is the oldest Christmas market in Germany. Dresden is one of the most affordable cities in Germany and great value at Christmas.

Specialties: Dresden stollen sweet bread, hot cider instead of mulled wine and Dresden rahmklecks, a local bread topped with savoury fillings.

Recommended tour: Dresden Advent tour is a city tour with stops at three Christmas markets plus you get to try the famous Dresden stollen and drink mulled wine.

Dresden weather in winter: Temperatures average 5°C / 0°C (high / low) in December.

Where to stay: Townhouse Dresden, located in the absolute heart of the Altstadt next to the Frauenkirche.

Hotels Near Dresden Christmas Market

In Dresden, you'll want to stay in the Altstadt to be within easy access to the Christmas markets and the most interesting city sights.

This is why I suggest staying at Townhouse Dresden. This hotel is located in the absolute centre of Altstadt, directly on Neumarkt which is the location of one of the Christmas markets and a short walk to Striezelmarkt.

Other Dresden Christmas Markets And Specialities

The Christmas season is huge in Dresden along with the surrounding areas in Saxony. The most popular Christmas events and markets are in Altstadt but it's worth spending time to get away from the centre for a few hours to experience other areas.

1. **Striezelmarkt** – The most popular and oldest Christmas market in Germany with Christmas stalls selling all kinds of gifts and

traditional and modern food. There are popular Christmas rides for the kids and a few for adults to enjoy too.

2. Frauenkirche – The traditional Christmas market in front of the stunning pale domed Frauenkirche is one not to be missed. It takes place from late November to Christmas Eve, along narrow Münzgasse.

3. Advent at Neumarkt – Also in front of the Frauenkirche, the Advent at Neumarkt takes over the entire pedestrian square until 23rd December 2022. This market is focused on artisanal crafts and delicious culinary classics.

4. Augustus Market – Across the river at the more modern Neustadt neighbourhood is the Augustus Christmas market on Albertplatz. Cross the historic Augustus Bridge towards to Ferris wheel to start exploring the markets.

5. Stallhof Advent Festival – Within the walls of the Dresden Royal Palace at Schlossplatz is a true craftsperson and traditional artisan Christmas market.

6. Postplatz Alpine Huts – An evening market with an apres-ski vibe specializing in hot drinks, mulled wine and hot cider. A very different Christmas market for over 18s only.

7. Neustädter Gelichter – Also across the river in Neustadt is an alternative take on the Christmas market with local handmade gifts, jewellery and vegan and vegetarian Christmas food.

8. Romantic Christmas Market – A less traditional and more decoration-focused Christmas market in the courtyard of the Taschenbergpalais.

9. St Nicholas Market – Located in Outer Neustadt, Dresden's hipster neighbourhood, this is a modern alternative to Dresden's traditional, classic Christmas markets.

FAQ

Question: Does Dresden have a Christmas market?

Yes! Dresden Christmas Market is the oldest in the world.

Question: How long does Dresden Christmas Market last?

The Christmas market lasts for 33 days from 23rd November to 24th December 2022.

Question: Which city is best for Christmas in Germany?

Dresden! Striezelmarkt is the oldest Christmas market in Germany. You can't beat the incredible beauty of Dresden's baroque Old Town (Altstadt) with the rebuilt Frauenkirche, Brühl's Terraces, the Opera and the incredible Zwinger. Dresden is one of the most affordable cities in Germany and great value at Christmas.

Question: How many Christmas markets are there in Dresden?

There are 9 Christmas markets in Dresden.

CHAPTER TWO

Vienna, Austria

Vienna is one of the most beautiful Christmas destinations in all of Europe. The historic architecture, wonderful museums and pedestrianized streets, all look stunning under Christmas lights and occasional snow.

The main Vienna Christmas Market is held in front of the Town Hall, a stunning backdrop to one of the oldest Advent events in Europe. But there are many other Christmas markets in Vienna and in this guide.

The Christmas markets span the city from the main market in front of the Town Hall to the magical Christmas Village at the Belvedere Palace.

The Christmas Village on Maria Theresien Square is huge, sandwiched between the Museum of Natural History and the Museum of Art, two of Vienna's most grandiose buildings.

Another favourite is the Christmas Market at Schönbrunn Palace or you could try the more modern Winter Market at the Museum Quarter.

Here are some of the Christmas markets in Vienna.

1. Vienna Christmas Market At Rathausplatz

Vienna's main Christmas market is a traditional Viennese Advent market located at Rathausplatz, Vienna's Town Hall.

The Christmas tree and park will be illuminated by Christmas lights and decorations. You'll find wonderful culinary treats, Viennese desserts, mulled wine, hot cider and hot chocolate.

Handmade gifts are popular and Christmas events include cookie-baking classes and candle-making.

Dates And Locations

Vienna Christmas Market dates: 19th November to 26th December 2022.

Opening times: 10am to 9:30pm. Closes at 6:30pm on 24th to 26th December.

Location: Rathausplatz – in front of the Town Hall.

Reason to visit: A traditional experience with incredible food, drinks, variety and atmosphere all in one of the most beautiful cities in the world. There is an ice skating rink in front of the Town Hall.

Specialties: International choirs, vanillekipferl Christmas crescent cookies, handmade decorations and the best food in Austria.

Travel tip: Book a long stay if you can. There is so much to see in Vienna, not just Christmas related but in every other way.

Where to stay: 25hours Hotel in the Museum Quarter as it's close to both the Town Hall and the Christmas Village on Maria Theresien Square.

Hotels Near Vienna Christmas Market

Vienna is designed in a series of rings that move out from the Danube canal. The area between the canal and the main ring road is called the Innere Stadt (Inner City), where you'll most likely want to stay.

Around the Musuems Quarter is also desirable as this is where you'll find many great cafes, restaurants and museums.

I suggest staying at 25hours Hotel as it's a 7-minute walk to the Town Hall Christmas market for those able to walk. It's 5 minutes to the market on Maria Theresien Square and 3 minutes to Volkstheater metro station for access to everywhere else in the city.

2. Christmas Village On Maria Theresien Platz

A short walk from the Town Hall, past the famous Volksgarten and Hofburg Palace, you'll reach Maria Theresien Platz.

This is the stunning square between the Museum of Natural History and the Kunsthistorisches Museum (the Museum of Art).

It's an incredible location at the best of times but during Christmas, it's home to the Christmas Village, a small Christmas market that also opens for New Year's.

A short walk from the Town Hall, past the famous Volksgarten and Hofburg Palace, you'll reach Maria Theresien Platz.

This is the stunning square between the Museum of Natural History and the Kunsthistorisches Museum (the Museum of Art).

It's an incredible location at the best of times but during Christmas, it's home to the Christmas Village, a small Christmas market that also opens for New Year's.

3. Belvedere Palace Christmas Market

Belvedere Palace is one of many historic palaces in Vienna with a beautifully curated formal garden. The Belvedere Christmas Village consists of 40 traditional market stalls.

This is a great Christmas market if you prefer a more traditional market with fewer crowds than the larger Christmas markets.

Belvedere Palace Christmas Market dates: 18th November to 26th December 2022.

Opening times: Monday to Friday 11am to 9pm. Saturday and Sunday 10am to 9pm. 24th December 11am to 4pm. 25th and 26th December 11am to 7pm.

Location: Belvedere Palace, Prinz Eugen-Straße.

Reason to visit: One of the more intimate Christmas markets in Vienna, situated on the grounds of an incredible palace.

4. Schönbrunn Palace Christmas Market

One of the most popular Christmas markets in Vienna, Schönbrunn Palace is an incredible baroque setting in which to celebrate Christmas in Vienna.

The Christmas stalls sell traditional handicrafts, wooden toys and an incredible array of Christmas decorations made of glass, wood, ceramics, paper and tin.

The culinary menu offers plenty of punch and mulled wine variations as well as Austrian delicacies such as kaiserschmarrn (sugared pancakes with raisins), sweet chestnuts or gingerbread.

Schönbrunn Palace Christmas Market dates: 19th November 2022 to 4th January 2023.

Opening times: 10am to 9pm. Closes at 4pm on Christmas Eve.

Christmas Day: Open 10am to 6pm.

Location: Schönbrunn Palace.

Reason to visit: Try the vanillekipferl biscuits dipped in hot chocolate.

5. Stephansplatz Christmas Market

In front of the iconic St Stephen's Cathedral is the very busy Stephansplatz Christmas Market where you'll find 40 Christmas stalls with Austrian products.

Located in the heart of Vienna's central pedestrian-only shopping district, you're sure to come across it at some point during your time in Vienna.

Stephansplatz Christmas Market dates: 11th November to 26th December 2022.

Opening times: 11am to 9pm. Closes at 4pm on Christmas Eve. Closes at 7pm on the 25th and 26th.

Location: Stephansplatz, at the corner of Graben and Kärntner Straße in the 1st district.

6. Art Advent Market On Karlsplatz

Art Advent is focused on art installations, music performances and children's events. Products available here are locally sourced and sustainably made. All the food served here is certified organic.

Karlsplatz Christmas Market dates: 18th November to 23rd December 2022.

Opening times: 12 noon to 8pm daily.

Location: Karlsplatz, near the Karlskirche.

Vienna is an incredible, historic city with beautiful architecture, world-class museums, unique stores, diverse cuisine and a progressive community. Vienna's Christmas markets have it all. History, tradition, quality and variety.

The city is very walkable, even in winter, and you're sure to come across other Christmas markets as you explore the city. If you're not able to walk, the city has an excellent public transport city that is accessible for all.

There are more Christmas markets in Vienna but those listed in this chapter are some of the best Austrian Christmas markets.

FAQ

Question: Where is Vienna Christmas Market held?

Vienna's main Christmas market is held at Rathausplatz.

Question: What date do the Christmas markets start in Vienna?

Dates vary but the main Christmas market at Rathausplatz starts on the 19th November and continues until the 26th December 2022.

Question: What time does Vienna Christmas Market open?

The Christmas market opens at 10am daily.

Question: What time does Vienna Christmas Market close?

The Christmas market closes at 9:30pm except on the 24th to 26th December when it closes at 6:30pm.

CHAPTER THREE

Manchester Christmas Markets 2022: Starts 11th November

Manchester Christmas markets are set to return in 2022 for another fun festive season. The Manchester market began in 1998 and has developed into one of the UK's largest and most popular markets, attracting thousands of visitors each day over the festive period.

Here, you'll find the dates, locations, opening times and what to expect during your visit.

There is a lot going on in Manchester this year with Christmas festivities, decorations, events, themed bars, rides and attractions.

Choose from family-friendly carousels and gift markets, or maybe you're heading out for a drink and some Christmas food.

The Christmas markets in Manchester take place in seven locations around the city. It's one of the busiest events in December, with new events and attractions being added each year.

Dates And Locations: Christmas Market Manchester dates: 11th November to 22nd December 2022.

The Winter Gardens Christmas market at Piccadilly Gardens and the Cathedral Gardens market will continue until the 3rd January 2023.

Christmas Day: Closed.

Opening times: 10am to 9pm.

Location: Piccadilly Gardens and 6 other locations listed below.

Reason to visit: Giant Santa and the Christmas light trail.

Specialties: Yorkshire pudding wraps, fried chicken, hot cookie dough, a gin bar and of course, gluhwein.

Travel tips: Each of the Christmas markets are within walking distance of each other. However, for those with mobility issues or if the weather is bad, you can take the free city bus that passes by most of the Christmas markets.

Where to stay: BrewDog Doghouse Manchester as it's only 3 minutes walk from Piccadilly Gardens.

Note that all of the Christmas markets are closed on Christmas Day.

Hotels Near Manchester Christmas Market

If you would like to stay near the Christmas markets, there are several hotels near Piccadilly Gardens or you can stay in the popular Northern Quarter, which is only a few minutes away.

The 7 Manchester Christmas markets are located in a loop that covers the city's cultural center.

In the center of this loop is the BrewDog Doghouse Manchester, where I recommend staying for its location and sustainability measures. This hotel is only 3 minutes' walk from Piccadilly Gardens.

7 Christmas Markets In Manchester

There are 7 Christmas markets in Manchester this year. Each has its own unique theme and atmosphere but you can find gifts, Christmas decorations, baubles, mulled wine and hot chocolate at each location.

1. **Piccadilly Gardens** – Known as Winter Gardens, this is the main Christmas market in Manchester that will replace the Albert Square Christmas Market in 2022.

2. **Cathedral Gardens** – Stays open until after the New Year. You'll find a huge range of handmade craft stalls here. This is also the location of the Skate Manchester ice rink.

3. **Exchange Square** – Look out for the famous Yorkshire pudding wraps at Porky Pig.

4. **New Cathedral Street** – A great spot for vegan products and food as well as cocktails and gin.

5. **St Ann's Square** – Expect to find Christmas craft stalls, Northern Quarter's Yard and Coop, Lakeland Burger Company and hand-pulled pizzas.

6. **King Street** – French-themed Christmas stalls and the famous gin bar with 100 varieties of gin.

7. **Market Street** – The place for local and regional artisan makers and traders.
8. **St Peter's Square** – This is not a Christmas market location, instead, it's where you'll find the Giant Santa that will be illuminated from the 17th November 2022.

If you are visiting from further afield, consider spending 3 or 4 nights in Manchester to experience the city's sights, attractions and cultural events.

FAQ

Question: What date is Manchester Christmas Market 2022?

11th November to 22nd December 2022.

Question: Where are the Manchester Christmas markets?

The Christmas markets are located at Piccadilly Gardens, Cathedral Gardens, Exchange Square, New Cathedral Street, St Ann's Square, King Street and Market Street.

Question: What time does Manchester Christmas market open?

The Christmas markets open at 10am daily.

Question: What time does Manchester Christmas market close?

The Christmas markets close at 9pm.

Question: Can I go ice skating in Manchester?

Yes, the Skate Manchester ice rink at Cathedral Gardens is open from the 31st October until the 3rd January.

Question: Do you have to book to go to Manchester Christmas markets?

No, you don't need to book; they are free to enter.

CHAPTER FOUR

Strasbourg, France

Strasbourg Christmas Market 2022 Dates: 25 Nov To 24 Dec

Strasbourg Christmas Market is known as Christkindelsmärik in the local Alsatian dialect. It is one of the most popular Christmas markets in Europe thanks to its fairytale location and world-famous mulled wine. It's also the oldest Christmas market in France. In Strasbourg, the Christmas markets and events are held in the city's grand squares and alongside the pretty canals lined with half-timbered houses.

Strasbourg is known as the Capital of Christmas and in 2022 the event is named "Allumons les étoiles", let's light up the stars.

Altogether there are more than 300 wooden Christmas chalets and huts selling handmade Christmas toys, decorations, artisans gifts, crafts and delicious food and drinks in Strasbourg at Christmas.

The Christmas markets in Strasbourg take place over more than 10 locations around the historic city centre known as the Grande Île district.

The largest and most popular is located in Place Kléber and this is where you'll find the city's enormous Christmas tree.

There are also many chalets around Place de la Cathedral, the centre square dominated by the extraordinary Strasbourg Cathedral.

Strasbourg Christmas Market dates: 25th

November to 24th December 2022.

Location: The main market is located at Place Kléber but there are other markets in the surrounding streets and squares.

Opening times: 11am to 8pm. Closes at 6pm on the 24th December.

Reason to visit: The 35 metre high Christmas tree in Place Kléber. Strasbourg has one of the oldest Christmas markets in the world as it first opened in 1570.

Specialties: A variety of aromatic mulled wines, tarte flambée, gourmet pretzels, raclette, Riesling, hot cider and Christmas biscuits.

Travel tips: Try to include a side trip to the beautiful Alsatian city of Colmar which is only 30 minutes away by train. If you would prefer to visit a few villages as well as Colmar Christmas market, you could take this popular tour with a local guide.

Where to stay: Two minutes from Place Kléber is Hannong Hotel, a lovely hotel with an in-house wine bar.

Hotels Near Strasbourg Christmas Market

To be near the Christmas markets, anywhere on the Grande-Île de Strasbourg would be suitable as this is where most of the markets are held, including the main market on Place Kléber.

I suggest staying at Hannong Hotel as it's only a 2 or 3-minute walk to Place Kléber as well as only 4 minutes to Petite-France, one of the most beautiful sights in Strasbourg.

The best hotels tend to book out early but in my guide to hotels near Strasbourg Christmas Market, I list several options that should help with your planning and booking process.

Things To Do In Strasbourg In Winter

Outside of the Christmas markets, there are plenty of interesting things to do in

Strasbourg in winter.

- Enjoying Alsatian cuisine is a huge part of a visit to the Alsace, a region that is known for its unique food, wine and cider.
- There is a wide range of cafes, restaurants, bars, delis and indoor markets where you can try the local specialties.
- As for sights and attractions, you can visit the numerous museums, historic houses, churches, galleries and concert venues.
- When the weather allows, you can take a boat ride along the famous canal that includes the unique experience of passing through a historic lock.

FAQ

Question: When does Strasbourg Christmas Market start?

The Christmas markets start on 25th November and continue until 24th December 2022.

Question: What time do Strasbourg Christmas markets open?

The Christmas markets open at 11am daily.

Question: What time do Strasbourg Christmas markets close?

The Christmas markets close at 8pm except on the 24th when they close at 6pm.

Question: Where is Strasbourg Christmas Market?

The main Christmas market is located at Place Kléber on the Grande-Île de Strasbourg.

Question: Is Strasbourg Christmas Market worth it?

Strasbourg has one of the best Christmas markets in Europe. The atmosphere is incredibly festive and the stalls sell quality decorations, handmade gifts and delicious food. It's well worth visiting if you can.

Question: Do you need tickets for the Strasbourg Christmas Market?

No, tickets are not required and it's free to enter.

Question: How many days do you need in Strasbourg?

I recommend at least 3 nights in Strasbourg to give you 2 full days to explore.

Question: Can you walk from Strasbourg to Germany?

You can walk from Strasbourg to Kehl in Germany by crossing the Pont de l'Europe pedestrian bridge over the Rhine River. It's a fun walk although it's an hour each way from Grande-Île de Strasbourg. I walked across the border one time but not during winter when it would possibly be too cold.

Question: Is Colmar or Strasbourg better?

Tough question! It's impossible to say if Colmar or Strasbourg is the better destination. Strasbourg is a larger city so has much more going on while Colmar is smaller, easier to get around and possibly prettier. You won't be disappointed either way.

CHAPTER FIVE

Prague Christmas Market 2022: Old Town Square From 26 Nov

Prague has always been one of Europe's most beautiful and intriguing cities. Prague Christmas Market is one of the winter highlights with its wonderfully festive atmosphere and beautifully decorated squares. Read on to find dates, locations and what to expect while you're there.

Winter in Prague is an incredible time to visit. There are generally fewer crowds, making it easier to get around, but the city is still busy with events and festivals. The Christmas markets are hugely popular, so visit in the morning if you'd like a quieter experience.

Prague Christmas Market 2022

Several Christmas markets await you in Prague. The biggest markets are at the stunning Old Town Square, the historic Wenceslas Square, and across town at Prague Castle.

1. Prague Old Town Square Christmas Market

If you can only make it to one Christmas market in Prague then I suggest visiting the Old Town Square. This is an incredibly beautiful, wide-open square, the oldest in Prague.

You'll find a diverse range of stunning architecture, the famous Astronomical Clock, and you can spot the iconic spires of the Church of Our Lady before Týn.

Prague Christmas Market dates: 26th November 2022 to 6th January 2023.

Opening times: 10am to 10pm.

Location: Old Town Square.

Reason to visit: The spectacular Medieval locations, views of Prague Castle and the festive old town decorations.

Recommended tour: Book your Prague Castle ticket in advance to avoid the queues. This is the most popular attraction in Prague.

Specialties: Although originating from Transylvania, chimney cake is hugely popular in Prague.

Food tour: For a more in-depth experience of Czech food, I highly recommend this Prague food tour, one of the best I've ever taken.

Where to stay: The Julius Prague is a highly-rated hotel that is near both the Old Town Square and Wenceslas Square.

Hotels Near Prague Christmas Market

Prague is a safe, walkable city with a great public transport system making it easy to get around.

The city is divided into numbered districts. Prague 1 covers much of the historic old town, including Old Town Square, Wenceslas Square, Charles Bridge and Mala Strana and Prague Castle on the other side of the river. These are all great areas to stay in Prague.

Prague has many fantastic neighborhoods outside of the old town, like Karlin, Žižkov, Vinohrady and even Holešovice if you want to get off the beaten path. But if this is your first time in Prague and you want to stay near the Christmas market, then I suggest staying in Prague 1.

I recommend staying at **Julius Prague** as it's less than a 10-minute walk to the main Christmas markets.

Alternatively, I suggest the Golden Star if you want to stay near Prague Castle. I stayed here on my last stay in Prague and the view over the city was incredible. This hotel is just down from the castle and a 25-minute walk to the Old Town Square.

2. Wenceslas Square Christmas Market

Another popular Christmas market in Prague is held at Wenceslas Square. This is a huge 14th-century square that looks up the hill to the National Museum.

The area is lined with chalets serving hot drinks and snacks like roasted chestnuts and traditional Czech cookies. There is a Christmas tree at the base of the square.

Wenceslas Square Christmas Market dates: 26th November 2022 to 6th January 2023.

Opening times: 10am to 10pm. Some food and drink chalets close at midnight.

Location: Wenceslas Square.

3. Prague Castle Christmas Market

The largest castle complex in the world holds a compact Christmas market in front of the

Basilica. It's free to enter. Be sure to check out the amazing views before you leave.

Prague Castle Christmas Market dates: 23rd November 2022 to 6th January 2023.

Opening times: 9am to 6pm.

Location: Prague Castle, in front of St George's Basilica.

Cost: Free entry.

4. Republic Square Christmas Market

Not far from Old Town Square is Republic Square. This is a quieter part of the city centre, but it's a popular shopping area thanks to the Palladium Shopping Mall.

You might also like to visit the Museum of Communism while in this part of the city and venture over to the EMA Espresso Bar if you're looking for great coffee.

Republic Square Christmas Market dates: 26th November to 24th December 2022.

Opening times: 10am to 10pm.

Location: Republic Square (Náměstí Republiky).

5. Tyl's Square Christmas Market

Cross over into Prague 2 in the Vinohrady district for the small Christmas market at Tyl's Square (Tylovo náměstí). This is a quieter area of Prague, just behind the National Museum.

Tyl's Square Christmas Market dates: 26th November to 24th December 2022.

Opening times: 10am to 6pm.

Location: Tyl's Square (Tylovo náměstí), Vinohrady, Prague 2.

6. Peace Square Christmas Market

Also in Vinohrady is the small market in Peace Square.

Peace Square Christmas Market dates: 20th November to 24th December 2022.

Opening times: 10am to 6pm.

Location: Peace Square (Náměstí Míru), Vinohrady, Prague 2.

7. Smíchov Christmas Market

Head off the beaten path to the Smíchov district for this Christmas market. This area is mostly a mix of business and shopping with some residences. I stayed in this area one time and was happy to catch the tram around the city. Prague 5 is mostly busy with locals.

Smíchov Christmas Market dates: 24th November to 24th December 2022.

Opening times: 10am to 6pm.

Location: Anděl, Prague 5.

Prague is home to one of the best Christmas markets in Czechia and all of Europe.

Visit Czech Republic is the official tourism website of Czechia. It's an excellent resource for finding things to do in Prague but also throughout the country. Find museums and galleries of interest, information on wine vacations and where to find the best Czech food.

FAQ

Question: When do Prague Christmas markets start?

Prague Christmas Market starts on 26th November 2022 and ends on 6th January 2023.

Question: Where is the Christmas market in Prague?

The biggest markets are at the stunning Old Town Square, the historic Wenceslas Square and on the other side of town at Prague Castle.

Question: Where to stay in Prague for Christmas markets?

If this is your first time in Prague and you want to stay near the Christmas market, then I suggest staying in Prague 1.

CHAPTER SIX

Zurich Christmas Market 2022 – 6
Old Town Locations

Zurich is the largest city in Switzerland and one of the most popular with visitors. You'll experience a wonderful combination of urban and nature while in Zurich.

The city has a gorgeous historic old town that sits on the shores of Lake Zurich while surrounded by snow-capped mountains.

Zurich Christmas Market is one of the highlights of a city break in Zurich in winter.

Zurich Christmas Market 2022

Zurich Christmas Market and Advent events take place all over the city from late November until New Year's Eve.

The festive **Christkindlimarkt** is held inside Zurich's central train station, while the traditional Christmas market in Niederdorf is Zurich's oldest and is known as the Village Christmas Market.

The Christkindlimarkt is where you'll find Zurich's famous Swarovski Christmas tree, a 16-metre high tree that is decorated with 7,000 Swarovski crystals.

Start your visit to the Niederdorf Christmas markets in Zurich with a stop at Mühlegasse followed by Hirchenplatz and ending at Grossmünster.

At Mühlegasse you'll be welcomed with the scent of cinnamon and mulled wine. At Hirchenplatz you can shop for Christmas gifts and Swiss culinary specialties while Grossmünster is famous for the fondue stands and delicious Swiss raclette.

Zurich Christmas Market: Niederdorf – the old town neighbourhood of Zurich that is known for its medieval streets, squares and cathedrals.

Zurich Christmas Market dates: 24th November to 24th December 2022.

Opening times: 11am to 9pm. Closes at 10pm on Fridays and Saturdays and 4pm on the 24th December.

Location: Between Mühlegasse and Grossmünster in the Niederdorf District. There are 5 other locations too.

Reason to visit: The mountain and lakeside landscapes and the stunning Swarovski tree.

Specialties: All kinds of food dipped in fondue, Swiss raclette, local handmade chocolate, artisan bakeries.

Travel tips: Switzerland can be very

expensive. If you're on a budget, consider shopping at the indoor food markets to prepare some delicious meals in your room for a reasonable price. Look for affordable street food options as you wander the old town and consider staying in an apartment to save on accommodation.

Hotels Near Zurich Christmas Market

One of the newest hotels in Zurich is Ruby Mimi Hotel. This is a modern boutique hotel that is light, bright and exceptionally well-located. The Ruby hotels originated in Vienna and it's great to see them expanding into Switzerland. This hotel is excellent value for money and is my top pick.

Other Christmas Markets In Zurich

There are a number of lovely Christmas markets in Zurich that you might come across as you walk around the city. Or you can hunt them down to experience those that are less touristy or with different themes and specialties.

- **Christkindlimarkt**: Zurich train station, Zürcher Hauptbahnhof. Closes on the 24th December. This is a great market to visit when the weather is poor as it is the only indoor Christmas market in Zurich.
- **City Christmas Market**: City Weihnachtsmarkt, Lintheschergasse. Situated on Bahnhofstrasse, Zurich's famous shopping street. This is one of the more modern Christmas markets in Zurich.
- **Urban Christmas Market**: Zürcher Wienachtsdorf, Sechseläutenplatz. Located next to the Opera House and Lake Zurich is a large market with 120 Christmas stalls with a large Christmas tree at its centre point. Note that this is a cashless market.
- **Regional Christmas Market**: Weihnachtsmarkt Münsterhof, Münsterhof. A market that specialises in regional products that are designed or manufactured in Zurich or the surrounding region. This a great

market to visit if you're looking for unique gifts to take home from Switzerland. This market closes on the 24th December 2022.

- **Musical Christmas Market**: Weihnachtsmarkt, Werdmühleplatz. Known for the Singing Christmas Tree, a choir performance by local children.

Zurich In Winter

There are many exciting things to do in Zurich in winter, most of which include visits to the incredibly beautiful mountains that surround the city.

Skiing, tobogganing, snowshoeing or cross-country skiing are some favourite sports with locals and tourists can easily participate too.

If winter sports aren't your thing then Zurich has some excellent world-class museums, gourmet experiences, indoor markets, spas and hammams.

If the weather is good, you can walk around peaceful Lake Zurich, one of the most beautiful lakes in Switzerland.

You won't be short of things to do during a short stay in Zurich.

If this is your first time in Zurich, I strongly recommend taking a short city tour upon your arrival in the city. This will give you an excellent overview of the city and an idea of places where you might like to revisit or spend more time exploring.

Zurich is a wonderful culinary destination and a great way to experience this is via a food tour.

There is plenty more to see in this part of the world during the Christmas period. Winter is a great time for exploring cosy Swiss cities, towns and villages. Several great places to visit are not far from Zurich so you could potentially include them in your trip.

FAQ

Question: What to do in Zurich on Christmas Day?

All of Zurich's Christmas markets are closed on Christmas Day, however, you can still enjoy the Christmas lights and decorations that will continue to be displayed. The city's museums and attractions are also closed on the 25th December. If the weather is good, I suggest taking the opportunity to visit some of the 1,300 open air works of art that are free to visit around the city.

Question: When do the Christmas markets start in Zurich?

There are 6 different Christmas markets in Zurich with most of them starting on the 24th November 2022.

Question: How do you say Merry Christmas in Switzerland?

In German speaking regions that include Zurich, the Swiss say 'Fröhlichi Wiehnacht'. In French speaking regions they say, 'Joyeux Noël', in Italian regions it's 'Buon Natale' and in the Romansh language it's 'Bellas festas da Nadal'.

Please be sure to follow all government travel guidelines and restrictions while in Zurich and elsewhere during your Christmas break in Switzerland. Be aware these may change at short notice so please continue to monitor the situation.

CHAPTER SEVEN

Budapest Christmas Market 2022 At Vorosmarty Square

Budapest has one of the best Christmas markets in Europe leading the city to be a popular winter break destination. Most visitors tend to stay 3 or 4 days but there are more than enough things to do to keep you occupied on a longer visit.

The main Budapest Christmas Market and Fair is open from November and continues past Christmas Day until New Year's Day.

There are multiple markets around the city, but the Vorosmarty Square Christmas Market is the most popular.

The second most popular is found in front of St Stephen's Basilica. Both are located in the central 5th district.

1. Vorosmarty Square Christmas Market

The main market is known as the Budapest Christmas Fair and is sometimes referred to as the Vorosmarty Square Christmas Market.

Vorosmarty Square is one of the busiest squares on the Pest side of the Danube River.

It's home to the famous Cafe Gerbeaud and Budapest's largest Christmas market.

The square is the starting point of Vaci utca, Budapest's main touristy shopping street which leads all the way to the Great Market Hall, the historic indoor food and shopping market.

Dates And Locations

Budapest Christmas Fair: The main Christmas market in Budapest.

Budapest Christmas Market dates: 18th November to 31st December 2022.

Opening hours: Generally from 10am to around 9 or 10pm.

Location: Vorosmarty Square in the beautiful 5th district of Budapest on the Pest side of the river.

Reason to visit: Budapest is vibrant, dynamic, affordable and one of the most beautiful cities in the world.

Specialties: Langos, goulash, kurtosh kalacs, salami, handmade lace and Christmas toys.

Temperature in December: December temperatures are typically around 4-8C during the day with temperatures occasionally dropping below zero during the night. These days, it rarely snows in Budapest, especially not in November or

December but rain is likely.

Hotels Near Budapest Christmas Market

I suggest staying anywhere in the 5th district as this is the most central neighbourhood. The 7th district is also well-located although this is the nightlife district so might not appeal to everyone. Buda is on the other side of the Danube and is quieter and generally more residential.

The Aria Hotel is one of the most exceptional in the 5th district and is located near both Vorosmarty Square and St Stephen's Basilica.

If you would prefer a budget hotel, the D8 Hotel is a great option and is only 2-minutes from Vorosmarty Square.

2. St Stephen's Basilica Christmas Market

There is a great Christmas market in front of the basilica from November to January. This is a smaller market but a wonderful location in historic Pest, in front of St Stephen's Basilica. From here, you're not far from the Hungarian Parliament, one of the most incredible sights in the city.

Dates And Opening Hours

St Stephen's Basilica Christmas Market dates: 18th November 2022 to 1st January 2023.

Opening hours: Usually 10am to 8pm and later on the weekends.

Location: Szent István tér (St Stephen's Square), in front of the St Stephen's Basilica in the 5th district.

Reason to visit: A small but cosy market with a small ice rink and Christmas tree in the centre.

Specialties: Langos, goulash, kurtosh kalacs, salami, handmade lace and Christmas toys.

Travel tips: For a small fee you can take the lift to the viewing platform at the top of the basilica. If you have time to visit the nearby parliament, it is free to visit for EU nationals and a small fee is payable for others (bookings are required).

3. City Park Ice Rink

Just across from Heroes' Square is Budapest's City Park. This turns into a winter wonderland over the Christmas and New Year period, with the park's lake being turned into an outdoor ice skating rink.

Ice skating has been a popular event here since the 19th century and continues to be so today. You can hire skates here or have your own sharpened if you need to.

4. Erzsébet Square Christmas Market

Erzsébet Square (Elizabeth Square in English) is located just steps from the Vorosmarty Square Christmas Market, yet they hold one of their own.

There are lots of things going on here as it's one of the most popular locations in

Budapest for holding events.

You'll find plenty of food trucks here and outdoor bars, which can get very lively at night. The square has a Ferris wheel for great views over Budapest.

5. Buda Christmas Market

The Buda side of Budapest holds its own small winter market with Christmas stalls that specialise in gifts, food and drinks like mulled wine.

Buda Castle is an interesting destination for tourists in this area and there are often markets and events within the Castle District as well as at the base of Castle Hill along the banks of the Danube.

These events change from time to time but it's worth stopping by and exploring the narrow streets of Buda that are very different to the wide open districts of Pest.

Hungarian Specialties

The Christmas markets in Budapest are a great place to try out traditional Hungarian specialties from the famous paprika-spiced goulash or chicken paprikash to quick and easy street food like langos or kürtőskalács (chimney cake).

You can get full meals at the Christmas market and there are plenty of benches and tables where you can sit but other items can easily be consumed while standing or walking around the markets.

A great introduction to Hungarian cuisine can be experienced via a food tour with a local guide.

Here are a few Hungarian specialties to try.

- **Langos** – A Hungarian speciality, langos is a deep-fried flat dough, usually topped with garlic, sour cream and grated cheese. This is not only popular at the Christmas markets in Budapest but at most European Christmas markets. If you don't get the chance to try it at the Christmas markets, you can get it at any time from Karavan on Kazinczy utca in the Jewish Quarter.

- **Kürtőskalács (chimney cake)** – This is the famous woodfired, sugar-coated cake that is prepared in a tubular shape. It is essentially a sweet dough that is rolled around a long, circular spit and cooked over coals then optionally topped with cinnamon or coconut. This dish originated in the Transylvanian region of Romania by ethnic Hungarians.

- **Beef goulash** – This classic Hungarian beef stew is known around the world. You can try it at the Christmas markets but you'll have much nicer versions at one of the nearby traditional restaurants. You can find vegetarian goulash at a few places in Budapest.

- **Chicken paprikash** – Another classic Hungarian dish, this slow-cooked chicken is served with a creamy paprika sauce, again probably best at a restaurant but you can get it from the

Christmas markets at Vorosmarty Square.

- **Stuffed cabbage** – A well-known and popular dish all around Central Europe, the Hungarians love it too and it's worth trying if you're looking for a hearty meal.

- **Chicken schnitzel** – It's not just the Viennese that love a schnitzel, the Hungarians have their own delicious version and this is a good option at the markets as you can easily eat it in sandwich form. If you can't find it at the markets, one of the best, cheapest and freshest versions can be found at Belvárosi.

- **Hungarian salami** – Mild and spicy versions of this Hungarian specialty are easy to come by in Budapest at any of the markets or supermarkets. It's great as a snack, for a picnic or to take home with you.

- **Smoked cheese** – There are plenty of locally made Hungarian cheeses worth trying while in Budapest. Smoked cheese is quite common in Hungary and a unique flavour that some love.

- **Pancakes** – Sweet and savoury pancakes are a great snack you can enjoy while taking in the festive atmosphere. This is a cheap street food that is commonly available.

- **Dobos torta** – This famous Hungarian cake layered with chocolate buttercream and topped with a thin layer of caramel. There are many Hungarian cake shops around Budapest but Cafe Gerbeaud in Varosmarty Square is one of the most famous and fanciest places to try it. You can order it takeaway or eat inside the beautiful, historic cafe. Alternatively, if you're on a budget, you can get a more affordable slice at Jégbüfé at Kígyó utca 4-6 in the 5th district.

- **Tokaj wine** – It's not just Slovakia where you can find the famous Tokaj wine region, it crosses the border into Hungary too. While this region isn't near Budapest, you can get this sweet wine at the Christmas markets and bars in the area. It's a lovely complement to a slice of dobos torta.

- **Palinka** – Every country has their own version of brandy and in Hungary, it is known as palinka. It comes in various fruit flavours and you can get shots from food trucks and bars. Of course, it's very strong so won't be to everyone's liking but you might find a flavour you like.
- **Unicum** – A strong herbal liqueur that is unique to Hungary, this is a very special drink that locals drink as an aperitif or digestif. First produced in 1790, the drink is bitter and in my opinion, tastes awful. It is most definitely an acquired taste. You can read about the drink's long history here.

Hungarian Traditions

Hungary has a long, rich history and cultural traditions. Budapest is a wonderful city to experience these and learn about its past and present.

Hungary celebrates St Nicholas an event that is called Mikulás in Hungarian. St Nicholas arrives in early December to give gifts to children.

Hungarians also celebrate Christmas by preparing traditional gingerbread. The gingerbread is flavoured with cinnamon and cloves and then decorated in folk motifs using red, green and white national colours.

FAQ

Question: When does Budapest Christmas Market start?

Budapest Christmas Markets starts 18th November 2022 and continues until 31st December.

Question: Where is Budapest Christmas Market?

Varosmarty Square and 4 other locations.

Question: What to buy at Budapest Christmas Market?

Handmade toys, jewellery boxes, lace and traditional food like langos, goulash and chimney cake.

Question: Is Budapest Christmas Market good?

Yes, it's one of the best in Europe. The atmosphere is incredibly warm and festive, the food is delicious and it is more affordable than markets in Germany, Austria and the UK.

CHAPTER EIGHT

Ljubljana Christmas Market 2022 – Sustainable Slovenia

If you're interested in sustainable travel during Christmas and want to avoid the mass consumerism common at more visited destinations, the Ljubljana Christmas Market is easily the best choice in Europe.

Slovenia is one of the most eco-friendly destinations all year round and in December the city focuses on supporting small, local businesses, zero waste products and organic Slovenian cuisine.

I've spent a lot of time in this city and it's a picturesque calm and quiet location with beautiful scenery and friendly locals happy to chat.

Christmas in Ljubljana in 2022 will include Christmas trees, decorations, and lights around the city centre with the main Christmas market taking place in Prešeren Square on the river.

Dates And Locations

Ljubljana Christmas Market dates: 25th November 2022 to 2nd January 2023.

Location: Prešeren Square, along the Ljubljanica River embankment and four other locations.

Reason to visit: One of the prettiest capitals in Europe. Strong focus on sustainability.

Specialties: Sustainable travel and products. Clothes by Slovenian designers.

Travel tip: Include a day trip to Lake Bled.

Winter events: Free music concerts. The Magical Forest.

Ljubljana weather in winter: Temperatures average 4°C / -2°C (high / low) in December.

Where to stay: Hotel Cubo in Ljubljana or find a Christmas hotels elseshwere in Slovenia.

Hotels Near Ljubljana Christmas Market

The Christmas markets in Ljubljana are located in Prešeren Square and along the Ljubljanica river. You can also find some festivities nearby in Congress Square (Kongresni Trg). I spent several months in Ljubljana and this area is by far the nicest neighbourhood to stay in.

This is why I recommend Hotel Cubo as it's very close to all the Christmas markets and other attractions in Ljubljana.

Ljubljana Christmas Market Specialities

Ljubljana, and Slovenia in general, is one of the most sustainable travel destinations in the world and this is reflected in the Christmas markets in Ljubljana.

- **The Land of Ice** – A Christmas event showcasing ice and snow sculptures by Slovenian and international artists.
- **Magical Forest** – Includes creative workshops where you can learn to make your own eco-friendly Christmas decorations.
- **Organ Grinders** – A familiar sight around the streets of Ljubljana over the winter months.
- **Free Music Concerts** – Held in Novi Square from the 14th to 25th December. There are other free concerts in Ljubljana too.
- **Honey Schnapps** – Delicious but strong. A Slovenian classic.
- **Christmas Decorations** – Unique abstract Christmas lights and

decorations line the streets of Ljubljana at Christmas.

Things To Do In Ljubljana In Winter

For a small city, Ljubljana has plenty to offer from incredible food, stunning castles and pristine nature.

Start with the most popular things to do in Ljubljana and then venture out for a day trip to Lake Bled and the mountains.

In the evenings, enjoy the atmosphere of the Ljubljana Christmas markets and Slovenian seasonal cuisine.

- **Ljubljana Castle** – The modern funicular is the quickest way to reach Ljubljana Castle and its wonderful views of the city and the mountains in the distance.
- **Ljubljana Dragon** – The symbol of Ljubljana is the fiery green dragon. You'll see dragons everywhere but the best dragons guard the popular Dragon Bridge.

- **Triple Bridge** – Three bridges cross the Ljubljanica River at Preseren Square in the historic centre of the city. It's the hub of the old town, bustling with buskers, food carts and visitors enjoying the view. The bridge was designed by Slovenia's most famous architect, Jože Plečnik.
- **The Central Market** – Also designed by Jože Plečnik, the Central Market is the home of Ljubljana's best fresh food and organic products. It's the perfect place to pick up picnic supplies if you're heading out on a day trip.
- **Preseren Square** – The main centre square in Ljubljana, unmissable for the pink Franciscan Church which dominates the square. This is the location of Ljubljana's main Christmas market.
- **Ljubljana Town Hall** – The baroque Town Hall is central to one of Ljubljana's most picturesque streets, lined with pastel-coloured buildings and baroque fountains.
- **Tivoli Park** – If the weather is sunny, take a walk through Tivoli Park to see

the outdoor photography exhibition and green open space.

- **Art Nouveau Ljubljana** – In the historic centre of Ljubljana you'll spot a number of impressive art nouveau buildings including Hauptmann House in Preseren Square, bold Vernik House and Urbanc House, the location of Ljbuljana's high-end department store.

FAQ

Question: Is there a Christmas market in Ljubljana?

Yes! Ljubljana is one of the most festive destinations in Europe.

Question: When is Ljubljana Christmas Market?

25th November 2022 to 2nd January 2023.

Question: Where is Ljubljana Christmas Market?

Prešeren Square.

CHAPTER EIGHT

Edinburgh Christmas Market 2022

Starts 25 November

Edinburgh's winter festivals combine Christmas and Hogmanay over the November to January festive period. It's one of the best times for visiting the city as you can pick and choose from a vast array of events and things to do.

Edinburgh Christmas Market is one of the most popular events and in this chapter, I list the updated dates for 2022 with opening times and locations.

While in Edinburgh, you can enjoy a ride on the Big Wheel, the Star Flyer or a traditional Christmas carousel.

Ice skating is always popular; you can hire skates if you don't have your own.

Edinburgh has two main Christmas markets: the traditional European Christmas market at East Princes Street Gardens and the Scottish Market on George Street towards St Andrew Garden.

Entry to the Christmas markets is free and no tickets are required. However, crowd control is in place to ensure everyone's safety. This means you may have to wait briefly during peak times, but it's generally fine.

Although everyone loves the Christmas stalls for eating, drinking and shopping, there are several other activities in the area.

Book tickets if you're interested in skating at the ice rink, taking a ride on the big wheel or finding your way through the Christmas Tree Maze.

Dates And Locations

Edinburgh Christmas Market dates: 25th November 2022 to 3rd January 2023.

Opening times: 10am to 10pm daily.

Location: East Princes Street Gardens in the Mound Precinct and along George Street in New Town.

Admission: The Christmas market is free and un-ticketed.

Big Wheel: Book tickets online.

Christmas Tree Maze: Located at West Princes Street Gardens.

Reason to visit: Special events, food, loads of drinks and a fun atmosphere.

Specialties: The Christmas Tree Maze and reindeer carousel.

Recommended tour: Take Edinburgh's most popular tour, a ghost tour of Edinburgh's vaults.

Travel tip: Hogmanay is a 3-day event that

includes Party at the Bells and the Torchlight Procession for which you must book tickets in advance.

Where to stay: Market Street Hotel is highy-rated hotel located in the Mound Precinct in the Old Town.

Hotels Near Edinburgh Christmas Market

Edinburgh Castle overlooks both the Old Town and the New Town and the area where it intersects, the Mound Precinct. This central area is where you'll most likely want to stay to be near the Christmas markets and the city's main sights and attractions.

You might also like to stay in one of Edinburgh's cool neighbourhoods like Stockbridge, Dean Village or even Leith on the waterfront.

I suggest staying at Market Street Hotel as it's a 6-minute walk to both East Princes Street Gardens and George Street.

Things To Do In Edinburgh In Winter

Visiting Edinburgh in winter made me seriously consider moving there to live. It's one of the UK's great cities and there are many interesting things to do all winter long.

- Of course, Edinburgh Castle is worth visiting all year round.
- Go skating at the George Street ice rink.
- Visit the Christmas Tree Maze at West Princes Street Gardens.
- Santa's Grotto is also at West Princes Street Gardens.
- The Festive Light Trail runs throughout the city over winter.
- Edinburgh Zoo has some interesting winter-specific events.
- The Royal Botanic Gardens are incredibly beautiful and a great escape into nature. The gardens are well worth visiting for what is effectively a living museum.

FAQ

Question: When does Edinburgh Christmas Market start?

The Christmas market starts on 25th November 2022 and continues until 3rd January 2023.

Question: Where is Edinburgh Christmas Market?

The Christmas market is located at East Princes Street Gardens in the Mound Precinct and along George Street in New Town.

Question: What time does Edinburgh Christmas Market open?

The Christmas market opens at 10am daily.

Question: What time does Edinburgh Christmas Market close?

The Christmas market closes at 10pm daily.

Question: Is Edinburgh Christmas Market free?

The Christmas market is free to enter and you don't need to buy tickets.

CHAPTER TEN

Krakow Christmas Market 2022

This is Poland's #1 Winter Market

Krakow Christmas Market is the most popular and the best Christmas market in Poland. It's located on Rynek Glowny, the 13th-century square in the centre of the old town. You can't miss the stalls as they sit between the famous Cloth Hall and the imposing St Mary's Basilica.

The market and old town location is a popular meeting place for locals and tourists alike. Many people visit after work and during the weekends leading up to Christmas day.

Krakow Christmas Market 2022

The Christmas market in Krakow is lined with timber huts where they prepare delicious grilled and smoked specialties and slow-cooked hearty soups and goulash.

You can also find handcrafted toys and Christmas decorations to take home or give as gifts.

Krakow Christmas Market dates: 25th November – 26th December 2022 with some stalls continuing into January for the Epiphany festival (until 1st January 2023).

Location: Rynek Glowny – the main old town square.

Reason to visit: It's a cool city with a younger crowd than in Germany and Austria, it's more affordable, there's a good chance of a white Christmas and there is always delicious cheap vodka.

Specialties: Oscypek smoked cheese from Zakopane served with cranberry preserve. Pretty crystal baubles. Sweet vodka based hot drinks.

Recommended tour: 4-hour Polish food tour or check our other recommended tours in Krakow.

Krakow weather in winter: Temperatures average 3°C / -4°C (high / low) in December. You might see snow if you're lucky.

Plan your trip: A list of resources to plan your Christmas holiday or winter break.

Travel tip: If you have time take a day trip to the Wieliczka Salt Mine, Auschwitz or to the mountains at Zakopane.

Hotels Near Krakow Christmas Market

Krakow in winter can be very cold, even in November and December. It's advisable to look for hotels near Krakow Christmas market to avoid spending too much time walking outdoors when the weather is poor.

However, once you arrive at the market you can warm up with mulled wine, hot soup or by standing around one of the heated areas.

I've visited Krakow several times and recommend visitors stay at the Puro Hotel.

Krakow Christmas Market Specialities

Krakow's market is heavy on food which is a great thing. There's so much to try!

These are just a sample of what is on offer and it changes every year but you can expect to see most of the following during the Krakow Christmas market period or even into January.

You can do your Xmas shopping at the market or browse the boutique shops in Kazimierz.

- **Smoked cheese** – A good option for vegetarians although it's sometimes wrapped and cooked in bacon!

- **Pierogi stalls** – Savoury stuffed dumplings with cheese, sauerkraut or various types of meat and sweet pierogies stuffed with berries and sweetened cheese.
- **Grilled meat stations** – Meat lovers can choose from local sausages, roasted pork knuckle, chicken kebab and loads of other grilled meats. You might want to avoid these if you're trying to travel more sustainably.
- **Soup** – There are a few vegetarian soups at the Krakow market; mushroom, tomato and cabbage. Plus you can get traditional goulash soup.
- Mulled wine from the huge barrels dotted around the market. Look out for signs saying grzane wino, hot wine in Polish.
- Polish dolls seem to be popular at the Christmas markets.
- Wooden toys and for some reason a lot of wooden kitchen gadgets.

Other attractions at the Christmas market include artisans working on their craft, singing, dancing and free concerts and the occasional appearance of Santa Claus for the kids.

Things To Do In Krakow In December

Krakow in December is vibrant and bustling with shoppers and visitors from around the world.

There is so much to see and do, visit museums or the countless churches, take a day trip to sombre Auschwitz or see the underground cathedral carved into a salt mine.

Krakow is also known for its religious history thanks to the strong presence of the Catholic church and with Krakow being the hometown of Pope John Paul II.

Krakow is a popular summer destination but it's becoming better known as a great break destination during the Christmas and New Year period.

It's a fun, young city, with so much history, great nightlife and laid-back cafe culture. While you're in Krakow, be sure to check out these things to do.

- **Wawel Hill and Castle** – Medieval royal castle and museum area. Try to see to visit at least one of the buildings in the museum complex.
- **Cloth Hall** – The huge building on the main square is home to little shops with handmade goods and unique gifts. It's free to walk through and have a look around.
- **Kazimierz** – The old Jewish Quarter is filled with cool cafes and bars. This is a great place to stay in Krakow if you want to be in a lively hipster neighbourhood.
- **Zapiekanka** – Eat a traditional Polish baguette/pizza topped with grilled mushrooms and cheese. Head to Plac Nowy in Kazimierz for the best. This is the best fast food in Poland!
- **Pierogies** – Don't miss out on eating some of the tastiest dumplings in

Poland. Sweet or savoury, pierogies are a must-try.

- **Sweet fruit flavoured vodka** – Poland is famous for all kinds of vodka (obviously) but in cafes around the main square like Cafe Camelot you can try some deliciously sweet, hot vodka, perfect for warming up in winter. They aren't as strong as you might imagine and vodka is inexpensive in Poland.
- **Brunch** – You might want to recover from a night of vodka drinking and eating with a delicious late breakfast at Bistro Charlotte. This modern cafe has fresh bread and baked items and excellent coffee.
- **Auschwitz** – If you have time, take a day trip to visit the former concentration camps at Auschwitz – Birkenau. Take a tour or get the bus from central Krakow (going by train is more complicated).

Krakow Tourism has information and more details about visiting Krakow on a Christmas break or winter holiday.

You can find out about museums, public transport, religious routes, Jewish heritage, Pope John Paul II, walking the Royal Route and many other attractions. They can also help with further questions regarding the Krakow Xmas market in 2022.

FAQ

Question: When does Krakow Christmas Market start?

25th November 2022.

Question: Where is Krakow Christmas Market?

Rynek Glowny, the medieval main square in Krakow.

Question: What to buy at Krakow Christmas Market?

Polish dolls are a particularly popular gift at the Christmas markets in Krakow. You'll also find handmade wooden items including children's toys, kitchen gadgets and Christmas decorations.

Question: Where to stay in Krakow for the Christmas markets?

Stay in Stare Miasto, Krakow's old town, if you would like to be near the Christmas markets.

CHAPTER ELEVEN

*A Quick Summary of the Best
Christmas Markets In Europe*

In this chapter, we will do a quick overview
of the different Christmas markets we have
seen in the previous chapters. Let's go.

Best Christmas Markets in Germany

1. Dresden – Dresden is a smaller city in the
east of Germany close to Prague, Berlin,
Nuremberg and Wroclaw. You could visit a

couple of these cities in one trip or stay and explore the historic city, its top museums and the oldest Christmas market in Europe.

2. Nuremberg Christmas Market – Nuremberg is a historic city with half-timbered houses, classic food and excellent museums. The market is one of the world's largest, oldest and most traditional. Nuremberg is popular with families as they have a market dedicated to children's activities.

3. Munich Christmas Market – One thing that puts Munich ahead of other Christmas market destinations is simply the number and variety of markets to choose from. Munich has everything from a Medieval-style market to a Pink Christmas market and the alternative Tollwood Winter Festival.

4. Bamberg Christmas Market – Known for its historic architecture that dates from the 11th to the 19th century, it's a wonderfully walkable city that can be visited in a day or two. The highlight is the nativity scene that changes from week to week throughout

Advent.

Best Christmas Markets In Austria

1. Vienna – One of the top reasons for choosing Vienna as your Christmas holiday destination is the huge number of Christmas markets that run at the same time. You can visit a different market each day, attend classical music concerts and choir singing, and visit all the typical Viennese attractions.

2. Salzburg Christmas Market – Salzburg is one of the most charming destinations in Austria, the pedestrianised centre is lined with boutique shops, you can walk through the Mirabell gardens to visit the palace and take the fortress funicular to visit the castle and enjoy the views over the city.

3. Hallstatt Christmas Market – Hallstatt is one of the most picturesque villages in Austria. Situated on a lake surrounded by snow-capped mountains, the scenery is breathtaking and the short-lived Christmas market adds to the charm.

Best Christmas Markets In The Uk

1. Edinburgh – Edinburgh has a great Christmas market with so much to do and see throughout November, December and after the New Year.

2. Manchester – The markets in Manchester are massively popular and the city is teeming with festivities throughout December.

3. Birmingham Christmas Market – This market is known as Birmingham's Frankfurt Christmas Market. It's the largest Christmas market outside of Germany and Austria.

4. Bath Christmas Market – The historic city of Bath is worth visiting all year round but especially for a winter break. Stay in a romantic bed and breakfast, explore the Roman baths during the day and then visit the festive markets in the evening.

Best Christmas Markets In Belgium

1. Brussels Christmas Market – For the most options for things to see and do in Belgium, visit Brussels and its lively Christmas markets. The main market is in Grand Place, the centre square lined with elaborate architecture with gold touches. The Grand Place is one of the most exquisite squares in Europe and the rest of the city is busy with Christmas and New Year's events.

2. Bruges Christmas Market – In spring, Bruges is known for its flower-lined canals but in winter, visitors focus on the Flemish architecture, an abundance of excellent restaurants, small museums and the popular Christmas market.

3. Ghent Christmas Market – Ghent is similar to Bruges in that the old town is built around canals lined with historic architecture. The difference is Ghent is quieter with fewer tourists so it's a great option if you want to experience a less crowded Flemish city.

Best Christmas Markets In Switzerland

1. Zurich Christmas Market – Advent events take place all over the city from late November until New Year's Eve. The festive Christkindlimarkt is held inside Zurich's central train station, while the traditional Christmas market in Niederdorf is Zurich's oldest and is known as the Village Christmas Market.

2. Lausanne – Bô Noël brings Lausanne to life during the four weeks of Advent by showcasing local creations in all their forms.

3. Basel Christmas Market – Basel is Switzerland's cultural and Christmas capital. The Christmas Market takes place across two main squares in the Old Town but the rest of the city is also decorated with Christmas decorations and pretty lights.

Best Christmas Markets In France

1. Strasbourg – The German and Alsatian influence mixed with French traditions and one of the prettiest cities in France make Strasbourg a great choice for a winter getaway. Strasbourg is rightly the most popular Christmas market destination in France.

2. Lille Christmas Market – Less well known as a Christmas market destination, Lille's market is compact but high quality. Lille is a great destination for foodies, museum-goers and those looking for a quieter winter city holiday.

3. Paris – Of course, the French capital has plenty to offer over Christmas and New Year. The Parisian Christmas markets are possibly more touristy and commercial than elsewhere but Paris is never a bad idea.

Best Christmas Markets In Poland

1. Krakow – Krakow's Christmas Market is Poland's most popular and best Christmas market. It's located on Rynek Glowny, the 13th-century square in the centre of the old town. You can shop for handmade gifts at the market or the boutique shops in Kazimierz.

2. Gdansk Christmas Market – The Gdansk Christmas Market is a stunning and unique market thanks to its Baltic Sea location. Forming part of Poland's Tricity region alongside Sopot and Gdynia, its Hanseatic history adds to the city's cultural appeal.

3. Warsaw Christmas Market – As Poland's vibrant capital, it's not surprising there are several Christmas markets in Warsaw. There's not just the traditional event in the Old Town Market Square but contemporary Christmas markets in Praga, Warsaw's alternative neighbourhood.

Best Christmas Markets In Italy

1. Bologna Christmas Market – Bologna is the foodie capital of the Emilia-Romagna region and, in my opinion, all of Italy. The Bologna market is a historic market in the city centre, with food events taking place over the entire winter period. If you love Italian food, visit Bologna.

2. Venice – Venice's Christmas market has artisan products like local Murano glass, traditional carnival masks and great tapas-style food. It doesn't hurt that Venice is one of the most unique and stunning locations in the world.

3. Milan Christmas Market – If you want a big city winter holiday with boutique shopping, classy Italian food and popular events, Milan has a lot to offer.

Best Christmas Markets In Northern Europe

1. **Copenhagen Christmas Market** – Copenhagen is home to a lovely Christmas market in front of the Town Hall or you can enjoy the family atmosphere at the Tivoli Gardens. Walking along the lit-up Nyhavn in December will round out your Danish experience.

2. **Stockholm Christmas Market** – A great city to visit all year round, Stockholm has excellent museums and galleries, a scenic archipelago, indoor shopping areas where you can stay warm and pretty decorations to get you in the Christmas spirit.

3. **Tallinn Christmas Market** – The most beautiful city in the Baltic States, Tallinn has one of the most well-preserved historic old towns with cobblestone streets and a huge Christmas market in the main city square. Tallinn is relatively affordable, there are lots

to do in the city and places worth visiting just outside. You can even take a day trip to Helsinki to experience the Finnish winter markets.

4. Riga Christmas Market – It may not be the most visited of cities but Riga is underrated and deserves more attention. Riga is cheap to get to and cheap once you get there. The city centre is walkable and charming, with cafe-lined streets and incredible Art Nouveau architecture.

5. Vilnius Christmas Market – The Vilnius Christmas Market (known as Christmas Town) is the highlight of winter in Lithuania, with Cathedral Square being home to one of the most stunning Christmas trees in the world.

Best Christmas Markets In Southeastern Europe

1. Zagreb Christmas Market – The Croatian capital Zagreb has probably the most traditional of the Balkans Christmas markets.

Zagreb is a quiet city, especially in winter, but it's cute and compact, perfect for a winter market break.

2. Sibiu Christmas Market – You might not think of Romania when it comes to Xmas markets but historic destinations like Brasov and Sibiu are charming and relatively cheap destinations with small markets and interesting food.

3. Tirana – Yes, even Albania has Christmas markets these days. I wouldn't go just for the market stalls but Tirana is always a fun city to visit and very unusual compared to elsewhere!

Those are my recommendations for Christmas markets to visit in 2022. As you can see, there are many options, so I understand it's a difficult decision!

I suggest picking one of the top 10 markets to start with or choosing your preferred country first and then taking it from there.

CHAPTER TWELVE

Tips

Christmas markets offer a sense of merriment and celebration, with markets of all shapes and sizes dominating entire towns and cities throughout the winter season. From massive events with over 300 individual stalls and daily nativity performances to smaller events aimed at those seeking a quiet getaway, there's something for everyone. Here are a few things you can do at these Christmas markets.

What To Eat At Christmas Markets

Schokokuss – the best way to describe this dessert is to take marshmallow fluff, then cover it chocolate, and eat a dozen. Really, these are inexpensive and are so light and fluffy. I get one almost every time I go to a Christmas market.

Bratwurst – Authentic German food is bratwurst and Rostbratwurst roasting continually. Each Christmas market does it a bit differently so try one wherever you go. You can get it with bread and I always load up on mustard and onions.

Kartoffellpuffer – Take potatoes, fry them. It sounds simple but they are absolutely divine. Usually served with applesauce (weird but good) or garlic sauce. Give these a try!

Gingerbread – Also known as Lebkucken, you'll find both soft and hard gingerbread sold. They also like to sell it in heart shapes, wrapped in plastic, with words written on the cookie. I can't say these are very tasty, but they are pretty!

Crepes – If you're in the mood for something sweet this is the perfect Christmas market food. Rolled up with nutella, cinnamon, sugar, or honey, anyone can get their fill from this simple classic.

Frikadella – One of my favorite foods at the Christmas markets are these hamburgers made with pork. Usually served with onions and mustard they make for the perfect hearty meal. Don't forget to grab some fries or pommes frites!

Candied nuts – the perfect warm Christmas market treat to pop in your mouth as you amble from stall to stall. These fragrant nuts will make you whip your head around as you walk past! You can also try roasted chestnuts aka "maroni" if you'd like as well.

Germknödel – This popular round dumpling is a German classic and usually filled with jam and topped with vanilla cream sauce. It's not overly sweet but a nice addition to your mulled wine.

Glühwein – You cannot go to the Christmas market without glühwein! I'm totally addicted to this hot, mulled wine made with spices. It will keep you warm inside as you drink this sweet liquid. Some markets also serve Feuerzangenbowle which is a mixture of punch and glühwein and topped with a rum-soaked sugar cube then set on fire. Go ahead, order two. If you're alcohol free you can also order kinderpunsch!

What To Buy At The Christmas Markets

Everything sheepskin is for sale – gloves, hats, rugs and more.

Keep your glühwein cup as a fun souvenir. If you want to keep with the alcohol trend, many stalls offer liqueurs in pretty bottles that are an excellent gift.

Most markets have their own traditions and

things for sale. For example, in Nuremberg they sell dolls made of dates! Most items for sale at Christmas markets are handmade and high quality. You won't necessarily find the cheapest items but you will find something special that will last.

Everyone deserves a winter wonderland break and Europe's Christmas markets make for the perfect magical escape. Christmas markets in Europe are some of the best memories of my life, and I'm already counting down the dates until next year!

WRAP UP

In conclusion, Europe's Christmas markets are a beloved tradition and a must-see experience for anyone looking to fully immerse themselves in the spirit of the holiday season.

With a rich history dating back to the 14th century, these markets offer a unique blend of traditional and modern, with each market offering its own unique traditions, decorations, and foods.

Visitors can expect to find stalls or chalets selling a wide range of handcrafted ornaments and crafts, local foods, and hot, mulled wine called Glühwein.

In addition to these treats, many markets also offer live entertainment, such as carolers and traditional dance performances, making them a festive and lively destination.

When planning a trip to Europe's Christmas markets, it is important to consider the best time to visit in order to avoid crowds and long lines.

Weekday visits, particularly on Mondays and Tuesdays, tend to be less crowded, and visiting during the day can also help to reduce the number of other visitors. In addition, it is important to bring cash, as most sellers only accept it at the markets.

Overall, a trip to Europe's Christmas markets is a must-do experience for anyone looking to fully embrace the magic of the holiday season. From the delicious foods and drinks on offer to the unique crafts and decorations, these markets offer something for everyone, and are sure to be a highlight of any trip to Europe.

Made in the USA
Las Vegas, NV
21 September 2023